BAMBIRAPTOR

and Other Feathered Dinosaurs

by Dougal Dixon

illustrated by
Steve Weston and James Field

PICTURE WINDOW BOOKS
Minneapolis, Minnesota

Picture Window Books
5115 Excelsior Boulevard
Suite 232
Minneapolis, MN 55416
877-845-8392
www.picturewindowbooks.com

Printed in the United States of America.

All books published by Picture Window Books
are manufactured with paper containing at
least 10 percent post-consumer waste.

Library of Congress Cataloging-in-Publication Data
Dixon, Dougal.
Bambiraptor and other feathered dinosaurs / by
Dougal Dixon ; illustrated by Steve Weston &
James Field.
p. cm. — (Dinosaur find)
Includes index.
ISBN-13: 978-1-4048-4013-3 (library binding)
1. Bambiraptor—Juvenile literature. 2. Saurischia—
Juvenile literature. I. Weston, Steve, ill. II. Field,
James, ill. III. Title.
QE862.S3D592 2008
567.912—dc22   2007040921

Acknowledgments
This book was produced for Picture Window Books
by Bender Richardson White, U.K.

Illustrations by James Field (pages 4–5, 9, 15, 17, 19)
and Steve Weston (cover and pages 7, 11, 13, 21).
Diagrams by Stefan Chabluk.

Photographs: istockphotos pages 6 (Rob Friedman),
10 (Matt Coats), 12 (John Swanepoel), 14 (Omar
Ariff), 20 (Tony Campbell); Frank Lane Photo
Agency 8 (Foto Natura Stock), 16 (Ariadne van
Zandbergen), 18 (S, D & K. Maslowski).

Consultant: John Stidworthy, Scientific Fellow of
the Zoological Society, London, and former
Lecturer in the Education Department, Natural
History Museum, London.

Types of dinosaurs

In this book, a red shape at the
top of a left-hand page shows
the animal was a meat-eater.
A green shape shows it was
a plant-eater.

Just how big—or small— were they?

Dinosaurs were many different
sizes. We have compared their
size to one of the following:

Chicken
2 feet (60 centimeters) tall
Weight 6 pounds (2.7 kilograms)

Adult person
6 feet (1.8 meters) tall
Weight 170 pounds (76.5 kg)

Elephant
10 feet (3 m) tall
Weight 12,000 pounds
(5,400 kg)

TABLE OF CONTENTS

WHAT'S INSIDE?

Feathered dinosaurs! These animals lived in many places in the prehistoric world. Find out how they survived millions of years ago and what they have in common with today's animals.

FEATHERED DINOSAURS

Dinosaurs lived between 230 million and 65 million years ago. Toward the end of the age of dinosaurs, some small meat-eating dinosaurs started growing feathers. The feathers helped keep them warm. Modern birds have a lot in common with feathered dinosaurs.

Beside a lake in what is now China, *Protarchaeopteryx* and *Sinosauropteryx* snarled at one another. *Microraptor* glided above them.

5

BAMBIRAPTOR

Bambiraptor was a tiny dinosaur. There probably were feathers and fluffy down all over its body. The dinosaur was a fierce hunter with sharp claws and teeth. It was able to fight the most dangerous small animals.

Fierce fighters today

The modern meerkat looks cuddly, but it is a fierce little fighter, like *Bambiraptor* once was.

Size Comparison

Bambiraptor had long fingers and sharp claws. It could catch and kill small animals such as scorpions.

7

MONONYKUS

Pronunciation:
mo-NON-i-kus

Mononykus may have had simple feathers and fluffy down, like a young bird today. The dinosaur's short arms were almost like wings. Each wing was tipped with a big claw. With the claws, *Mononykus* dug up food such as insects.

Big claws today

The modern aardvark scratches its way into termite nests, just as *Mononykus* might have done long ago.

Size Comparison

As *Mononykus* scratched into a termite nest, the dinosaur caught escaping insects in its jaws and swallowed them whole.

9

BEIPIAOSAURUS

Pronunciation:
bay-pyow-SAW-rus

Beipiaosaurus was a big feathered dinosaur. The dinosaur was covered in fluffy down. It had long claws for reaching into trees and pulling down branches. *Beipiaosaurus* ripped the leaves from the branches and then ate them.

Leaf-eaters today

The modern sloth is smaller than *Beipiaosaurus* was, but the sloth uses its claws to gather leaves, too.

Size Comparison

Beipiaosaurus had a beak that it used to pull leaves from tree branches.

Troodon had a big brain and large eyes. The dinosaur's long legs and sharp little teeth made it a fast and fierce hunter. Curved claws stretched from each of its toes. *Troodon* used the deadly claws to kill its prey.

Fierce hunter today

The modern secretary bird is about the same size and shape as *Troodon* was. The secretary bird hunts mostly on foot and uses its beak and claws to kill.

Size Comparison

Troodon's big eyes were perfect for hunting. It may have hunted at night as well as during the day.

13

PROTARCHAEOPTERYX

Protarchaeopteryx looked like a bird, but it could not fly. The dinosaur used its wings and tail feathers for show. When open, the tail feathers were fan-shaped. The feathers may have been brightly colored and used to signal to other animals.

Bright feathers today

Like *Protarchaeopteryx* once did, the modern bird of paradise uses its colorful feathers for show.

Size Comparison

14

Protarchaeopteryx leaped into the air to catch flying insects, sweeping them into its mouth with feathered wings.

15

SINOSAUROPTERYX

Pronunciation:
SIGH-no-saw-OP-ter-iks

Sinosauropteryx was covered from head to tail in fine, fuzzy down. It ran along the ground, searching for insects, lizards, and little mammals to eat. But *Sinosauropteryx* watched for bigger hunters. It would have made a tasty meal for a meat-eater!

Hiding hunter today

Like *Sinosauropteryx* once did, the modern elephant shrew hunts along the ground but hides from big hunters.

Size Comparison

Before *Sinosauropteryx* ate, it checked to make sure other hunters were not watching.

MICRORAPTOR

Tiny *Microraptor* was one of the smallest dinosaurs. *Microraptor* was so light that it could glide between the trees on its feathered wings. The wings stretched outward from each of its arms and legs.

Gliding wings today

Like *Microraptor* once did, modern flying squirrels glide from tree to tree, using the skin between their outstretched legs as gliding wings.

Size Comparison

Microraptor did not fly like a modern bird. Instead, it glided short distances from tree to tree.

DEINONYCHUS

Pronunciation:
die-NON-i-kus

Deinonychus was a very fierce dinosaur. The animal had a large, curved claw on each of its hind feet. *Deinonychus* hunted in groups. The dinosaur kicked at prey with its hind feet. The sharp claws made deep cuts.

Feeding a family today

Like *Deinonychus* once was, modern eagles are fierce hunters. They also look after their young.

Size Comparison

20

Deinonychus brought food to its babies. As the babies grew, feathery down covered their bodies.

21

Where Did They Go?

Dinosaurs are extinct, which means that none of them are alive today. Scientists study rocks and fossils to find clues about what happened to dinosaurs.

People have different explanations about what happened. Some people think a huge asteroid that hit Earth caused all sorts of climate changes, which caused the dinosaurs to die. Others think volcanic eruptions caused the climate change and that killed the dinosaurs. No one knows for sure what happened to all of the dinosaurs.

Glossary

beak—the hard front part of the mouth of birds and some dinosaurs; also called a bill

claws—tough, usually curved fingernails or toenails

down—the soft, fluffy feathers of a dinosaur or bird

glide—to fly slowly without using any motion

insects—small, six-legged animals; they include ants, bees, beetles, and flies

mammals—warm-blooded animals that have hair and drink mother's milk when they are young

prey—an animal that is hunted and eaten for food

signal—to make a sign, warning, or hint

To Learn More

More Books to Read

Clark, Neil, and William Lindsay. *1001 Facts About Dinosaurs.* New York: Dorling Kindersley, 2002.

Dixon, Dougal. *Dougal Dixon's Amazing Dinosaurs.* Honesdale, Penn.: Boyds Mills Press, 2007.

Holtz, Thomas R., and Michael Brett-Surman. *Jurassic Park Institute Dinosaur Field Guide.* New York: Random House, 2001.

On the Web

FactHound offers a safe, fun way to find Web sites related to topics in this book. All of the sites on FactHound have been researched by our staff.

1. Visit *www.facthound.com*

2. Type in this special code: 1404840133

3. Click on the FETCH IT button.

Your trusty FactHound will fetch the best Web sites for you!

Index

Look for all of the books in the Dinosaur Find series: